# TRAINS

by Rose Lewis

Pioneer Valley Educational Press, Inc.

# TABLE OF CONTENTS

Long ago there were no cars, airplanes, or trains. People traveled in carriages or wagons pulled by horses. When the first trains were invented, they were also pulled by horses. The very first railroads went only a short distance.

4

The first steam-powered train was built in 1804. It was called a **locomotive**.
To make steam, workers shoveled wood or coal into a firebox that heated water in a boiler.
The boiling water turned to steam.
The steam created **pressure**, which moved rods to turn the wheels of the train.

In the early 1800s, people in the United States began moving out West where it was less crowded. They needed better **transportation** to travel across the country, so they built longer railroads for trains.

It was hard to lay tracks in many places. Tracks needed to pass through thick forests and tall mountains. Workers had to blast tunnels through mountains and build bridges over rivers.

The United States government gave
the railroad companies land grants in the West.
This helped the railroad companies
build more tracks.

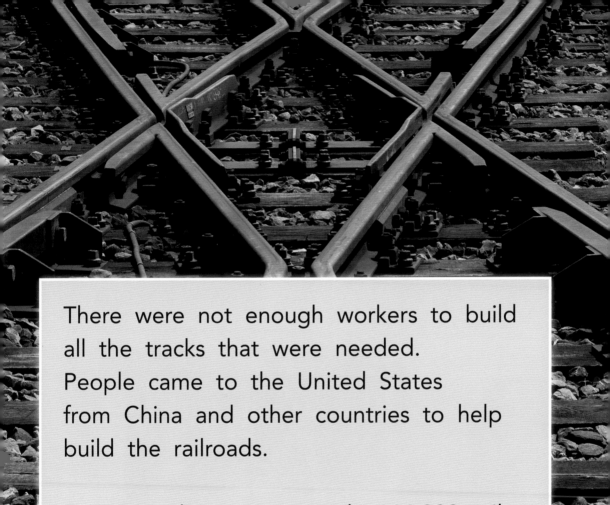

There were not enough workers to build all the tracks that were needed. People came to the United States from China and other countries to help build the railroads.

By 1890, there were nearly 164,000 miles of train tracks across the country. It became easier and faster to travel long distances.

The first passenger trains were dirty and crowded. Later, railroad companies added sleeping and dining cars to some trains so people could sleep and eat meals as they traveled. Trains became a popular and comfortable way to travel.

As more and more roads were built, people started driving cars instead of traveling by train. Today, in most parts of the United States, cars are the most popular way to travel. People use cars to go to work, to travel on vacation, and to visit friends and family. The wide use of cars is making our roads crowded and creating **pollution**.

14

Airplanes have become a popular way to travel long distances because they are much faster than cars and trains. A flight across the country takes only a few hours, but a train ride can take a few days.

Now, fewer people travel long distances by train. Trains are still used to move large amounts of **cargo** across the country.

Today, there are still some trains powered by steam engines. Most trains are powered by **diesel** engines or electric engines.

Trains carry people and cargo. A freight train carries cargo from place to place. A freight train may carry vegetables from farms to towns and cities. It may also carry mail, lumber, coal, cars, grain, and animals.

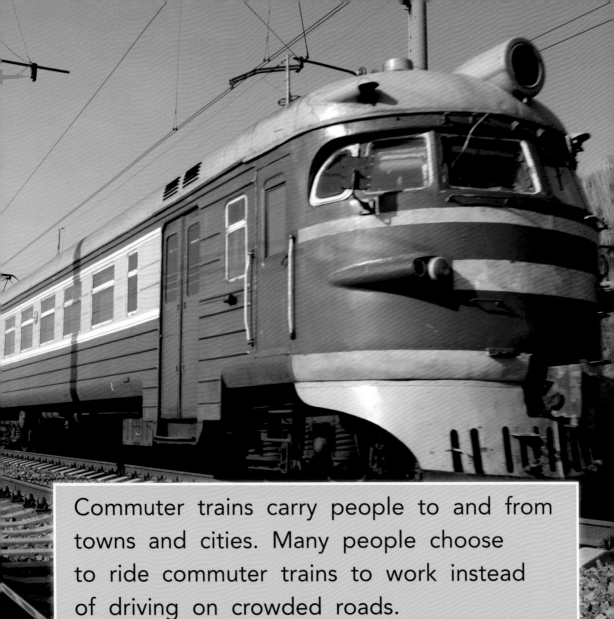

Commuter trains carry people to and from towns and cities. Many people choose to ride commuter trains to work instead of driving on crowded roads.

A subway, or metro train, carries people around a city.

# TRAINS IN THE FUTURE

The cost of energy is increasing,
and the amount of pollution is growing.
Trains use less energy and create less pollution
than cars, trucks, and airplanes.

New trains are being built that can travel
at very high speeds.

In the future, trains may become a popular way
to travel long distances again.

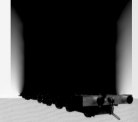

**cargo**: the goods or merchandise carried on a train, ship, airplane, or vehicle

**diesel**: an internal combustion engine that burns heavy oil

**locomotive**: an engine powered by steam, diesel, or electricity, for pulling or pushing trains along a railroad track

**pollution**: putting harmful substances or products into the environment

**pressure**: the exertion of force upon an object

**transportation**: the act of moving people and goods

# INDEX